Smiling on the Outside Dying on the Inside

Freedom from Autoimmunity and Chronic Illness

DEBBIE BILEK

2nd Edition Revised

Smiling on the Outside, Dying on the Inside © 2017, 2020
by Debbie Bilek.
All rights reserved. Printed in the USA.
2nd Edition

Published by Author Academy Elite
P.O. Box 43, Powell, OH 43065
www.AuthorAcademyElite.com

All rights reserved. This book contains material protected under International and Federal Copyright Laws and Treaties. Any unauthorized reprint or use of this material is prohibited. No part of this book may be reproduced or transmitted in any form or by any means electronic or mechanical, including photocopying, recording, or by any information storage and retrieval system, without express written permission from the author.

Identifiers:

Library of Congress Control Number: 2020906776
Paperback: 978-1-64746-240-6
E-book: 978-1-64746-241-3

Available in paperback, e-book, and audiobook.

All Scripture quotations, unless otherwise indicated, are taken from the Holy Bible, New International Version®, NIV®. Copyright © 1973, 1978, 1984 by Biblica, Inc.™ Used by permission of Zondervan. All rights reserved worldwide.

Scripture quotations marked NKJV, KJV, NLT, HCSB, BSB, and ESV are taken from https://biblehub.com. Accessed 2017.

Any internet addresses (websites, blogs, etc.) and telephone numbers printed in this book are offered as a resource. They are not intended in any way to be or imply an endorsement by Author Academy Elite, nor does Author Academy Elite vouch for the content of these sites and numbers for the life of this book.

Book design by Jetlaunch.
Cover design by Debbie Cloud, The Cloud Company.

Also by Debbie Bilek

Strategies from Heaven; Contending for the Impossible

12 Strategies from Heaven for the Ekklesia

Dedication

This book is dedicated to my Lord and Savior, Jesus Christ. He is my everything. Without Him, I would surely not be standing here today testifying of His goodness and grace. Thank You, Lord, for not giving up on me. Thank You for never turning Your face from me during all the years of suffering and pain. Thank You for walking each step of my journey with me. Though I couldn't see You or feel You at times, You were there. You are so faithful. I give You my life. Use me always for Your glory, Lord!

This book would not have been possible without the loving, constant support of my faithful husband, Bill. He has stood by my side through the good and the bad for over thirty-two years. He is my best friend, my soul mate, the father of our children, and the love of my life. Thank you, Bill, for being my rock, my steady, my support, and my strength. I will love you forever!

Table of Contents

Acknowledgments ix
Chapter 1: Today Is the Day that I Live or Die . . 1
Chapter 2: Survival Mode 5
Chapter 3: Sick and Miserable 9
Chapter 4: Words of Life 13
Chapter 5: Bitterness, Anger, and Unforgiveness . . 18
Chapter 6: The Change 23
Chapter 7: From Chronic Pain to Chronic Praise . . 29
Chapter 8: Living Out the Call and Destiny . . . 36
Chapter 9: He Hears the Cries of Your Heart . . 42
Chapter 10: Total Transformation 48
About the Author 55

Acknowledgments

Without my three beautiful children, this book would not exist. Thank you, Ariana, Brennan, and Rebekah, for giving me something to fight for, something to live for. Thank you for your gracious, loving devotion despite my shortcomings as a mom. You are three of the strongest human beings I know. I love you more than words can say. I am in awe of the world-changers you are becoming! May you serve God always!

Special thanks to Dr. Ryan McGaughey of Atascadero, California. Dr. McGaughey is the most caring, compassionate doctor I have ever met. From the day I walked through his door he was determined to see me whole and well. He did not care that I could not pay him what he was worth or that I had tried every other doctor and treatment out there. He cared about getting me healthy. Dr. McGaughey taught me about nutrition and educated me on my diseases. He spent hours researching my illnesses, and provided continual hope. Thank you, Dr. McGaughey, for praying for me as you treated me, and for not giving up through the trial and error process. You are a gift from God, and I know He has amazing things in store for you and your family.

With loving thanks to the treasured gift that God brought to me when He knew I was at my lowest. Thank you, Delinda Redding, for walking into my life at the perfect time when I needed a special friend, a kindred spirit, a running mate. You were that timely blessing in the storm who encouraged me, realigned me, focused me, kicked me in the rear when I needed it, and reached in to pull out the gold in me.

And lastly, a huge thank you to my friends and co-laborers in Jesus at the North County Healing Rooms. Thank you for standing by my side, for loving me, and for calling out my true identity. Thank you for not giving up on me when I was broken, hurting, lost, and deceived. You are rare and precious gems. God sees your hearts and says, "Well done, my good and faithful ones, well done." You carry Jesus, and you carry Him well. You are everything that "Love" should look like and I am ever grateful to have been allowed to journey with you for such a time as this.

CHAPTER 1

Today Is the Day that I Live or Die

The pain raged inside my head! I glanced at the ten bottles of prescription medication sprawled across my nightstand. They were staring back at me, almost as if calling my name. I leaned over and reached for a bottle of pills. I opened the bottle… I closed the bottle. I opened the bottle again. I lifted it up to my mouth. Something stopped me. I violently flung it at the wall. Pills scattered across the room as the container shattered upon impact. My heart screamed inside of me. I was at the end, and I knew it. I swiped my hand across the nightstand, crashing the remaining nine bottles of medication to the floor. I rolled over, pulled the covers up tight around my neck, placed a pillow over my head, and cried myself to sleep.

It was a cold, rainy night. I had been battling pain—resulting in depression—for quite some time. I had been sick for over twenty years with autoimmune disorders, chronic illness, and migraine headaches. I was exhausted and just wanted to die. I had been listening to the lies of the one who comes to "steal, kill, and destroy" as stated in John 10:10 of the Bible. I was hearing over and over in my head: *You are worthless. You will always be sick. You are a burden to your family. You will never be good for anything. You are just trying to survive. You might as well give in and die.* I was fighting for my very life. The sound of the enemy was far outweighing the sound of any truth I had ever known.

My husband was asleep in the next room and did not know the extent of my inner struggle. He had always been so faithful, patient, and kind. I knew I was hurting him. I had asked him to sleep in the other room for a few nights as I often did when I was ill, in pain, and just needed the bed to myself. He was my rock, my gentle and steady support. He was the love of my life who had cared for me and loved me through nearly three decades of the good and the bad; though lately it seemed to be more bad than good. The guilt continued welling up inside of me. How could he continue to love me in this condition? He went to work each day, all day, and then came home to do laundry, dishes, yard work, and all the other chores that running a household and family require.

I slept fitfully through the night. I stayed in bed as my husband got ready for work the next morning. I listened for my sweet, loving daughter Rebekah to leave for school. Of our three children, only Rebekah, our youngest, was living in the home since she was still in high school. When I knew they were gone, I dragged myself out of bed, showered, and packed a bag. I wrote a carefully scripted note to my family telling them of my love for them, how much they meant to me, and that I was leaving for a few days. I wanted them to know that no matter what happened that day, I loved them.

I climbed into the car and began driving north. My head was throbbing with a migraine, and it was pouring down rain. I screamed to God, "Today is the day that I live or die!" I cried for most of the trip, begging God to allow the car to crash and take my life. I was weary and just wanted to sleep… forever. I actually pleaded with God to allow my car to veer off the road, not wanting to hurt anyone else, but allowing me to die and go home to heaven. God spared my life in that moment, even though my thoughts and emotions continued to partner with the lies of the enemy of my soul.

> *I wanted them to know that no matter what happened that day, I loved them.*

The trip was extremely significant. By that time in life, I had been diagnosed with interstitial cystitis, migraine headaches, fibromyalgia, chronic fatigue syndrome, Hashimoto's thyroiditis, and Sjögren's syndrome. I was physically unable to drive more than an hour alone because I didn't have the energy or the stamina. I was weak, tired, in constant pain, and had little endurance. I was foolish to have even embarked on a journey of that distance by myself. I knew the trip would either kill me or be the beginning of a new chapter in my life.

The previous December, my son, who was attending college back East, had been home for Christmas break. While in California, he traveled with some buddies to a place called Bethel Church in Redding. He came home with stories of witnessing healing miracles during his time there. Friends of mine had also been talking about this place called Bethel. I browsed through the church website and watched numerous testimonies of healings that had taken place there. I thought if I could just get there, I would be healed. So that was the morning I got up, showered, packed a bag, left a note, got in the car, and began the long journey north.

As I drove, I could barely see out the window and I wondered if the tears of my soul were heavier than the rain pouring down my windshield. I don't think I have ever cried so hard in my entire life. I had not traveled that distance in over twenty years without my husband or my children, and I had just left all that I knew behind, not knowing if I would live or die. I screamed at God. I yelled at Satan. I begged God to take me home.

If I could just get there, I would be healed.

God overwhelmed me with His grace and mercy that day. Seven hours later, I arrived in Redding, California, checked into a hotel, and began my three-day journey of hashing it out with God. A horrible feeling swept over me. I was alone in a hotel room in a strange city, surrounded by not one soul that I knew or cared about. I had never felt so alone in my entire life. I got into bed and sobbed, until sleep overtook me.

CHAPTER 2

Survival Mode

I wish I could tell you that I was completely healed at Bethel and stepped into a fairytale world of my "happily ever after," but that was far from the case. Though the people were extremely kind, loving, and attentive to me, my physical state remained unchanged. It actually took me two days to make the drive home because I was feeling sicker than the day I left. My spirits were low, but I kept talking to God and found myself beginning to hear His voice, not audibly, but in my spirit. I felt His grace on my life, despite my circumstances. I anticipated that this was the start of a new season. Something had shifted during my time at Bethel, but I didn't quite know what. By the time I arrived back to my house, I had a newfound confidence that I would somehow keep on living.

Once home, I began a further decline in my physical health. My shoulder began having problems, and I was facing yet another surgery. After one failed surgery and a diagnosis of reflex sympathetic dystrophy, I was told by three different surgeons that I would eventually lose the use of my left arm. Life continued, but my morale was dropping more and more with each new day. I could not wait for the sun to go down so I could crawl into my warm, cozy bed each night. My bed had become my haven, my safe space, my solitude, my hiding place. I had grown to love it more than life itself.

I did not share my struggles with many people. It felt strange. I looked okay on the outside, so when I would tell somebody I was struggling, the usual response was, "You don't look sick!" I didn't know what to do with that response. Inside, my body was screaming in pain. I was exhausted and miserable. I felt as if I was dying a slow death. Yet on the outside, I smiled, sucked it up and went on with life as best I could, living in my own little world of secret pain and suffering.

The weeks were consumed with doctors' appointments and sleep. I had been on a quest for years to find out exactly what was wrong with me. My body hurt all over and I had chronic migraine headaches more days than not. I found myself sleeping ten to twelve hours a night and still needing to sleep during the day. The only time I did not feel pain was when I was sleeping, but sleep did not come easy. It was restless, interrupted, and far from peaceful. I went from doctor to doctor seeking answers, always being sent away with more drugs to simply manage the pain and symptoms. I wanted answers, not medication, but there were none to be found. I would climb back into my car after each

> *"You don't look sick!"*

appointment, despair welling up in my heart, and bawl the whole way home until I could eventually escape once again to my bed.

I had been to numerous doctors and specialists over the years. I had tried every medication and homeopathic remedy known to humankind. I had received acupuncture, chiropractic care, myofascial release, massage therapy, physical therapy, and a whole array of naturopathic treatments. I had spent thousands of dollars chasing rabbit trails. I had read articles, researched my diseases, cried out to God for healing, and done everything I knew in my power to do. I had been prayed for by so many incredible people. Yet I remained sick. I read and re-read the Word of God. I knew there was a God out there who loved me and could heal me with just a spoken word or a touch from heaven. I asked, "Why, God? Why?" I must confess that it was extremely difficult to see God as a loving Father when He allowed me such pain.

I had read the Bible story in Matthew 9:20-22, where a woman endured a severe health challenge. She had been bleeding for twelve long years. As word came that Jesus was passing through her town, she knew that if she could just touch the hem of His robe, she would be healed. This woman was full of faith as she pressed through the crowds, grabbed the end of Jesus' garment, and received her healing. This biblical account resonated in my spirit and gave me hope. Many times through the years I would catch myself thinking, *If I could just touch the hem of His garment...*

I watched my kids suffer year after year, having to endure the wrath of a sick mother, and it was almost more than my heart could bear. I reached out for prayer every chance I was given. I was frustrated and sad. I became hopeless. I loved the Lord and knew that He loved me. I had been living my life for Him and was doing my best to serve Him. I knew what the Word of God said about healing, but did I really believe it? I wanted desperately to believe, but I had been prayed for repeatedly with no results. Each time ended in disappointment for both me and the person praying for me. I had given up believing I would ever be healed. I began partnering with each new diagnosis, accepting it, and walking further and further into it as I agreed with the words spoken over me by well-meaning professionals.

If I could just touch the hem of His garment...

Many of you have had words spoken over you and diagnoses given. What have you done with them? Personally, I embraced each one as it came. I walked deeper and deeper into every new illness until survival seemed impossible. I was just waiting for the day I would die. There was no life in my soul, no spring in my step, no joy in my heart. Everything was dark, a burden, a struggle. Life stunk! I had written love letters to my children for them to read after I passed away. It seemed death was lurking ever nearer, ready to lunge me into eternity. Secretly, I could not wait for that to happen!

CHAPTER 3

Sick and Miserable

One day while lying alone in bed with my thoughts, I wondered, *How did I get here?* Thinking back over my adult life, my college years had been full of joy, yet persistent with trials. It was during my first year away from home, while studying at California Polytechnic State University in San Luis Obispo, California, that I began my personal relationship with Jesus Christ. I accepted Him as my Lord and Savior and embraced my newfound faith. That same year I received my first official diagnosis of having an autoimmune disease.

At eighteen years old, I'm not sure I fully understood what an autoimmune disease was, let alone what having a chronic illness entailed. I knew I was sick. I endured daily pain, and I knew my symptoms were real. Life went on as I managed my diseases as best I could. I got married to my college sweetheart, graduated from Cal Poly, and began my first "real" job in the professional world. Three years later I gave birth to a precious baby girl. Another three years passed and I gave birth to a sweet baby boy. A few years after that we adopted another gift from God—a beautiful, active toddler. Life was full and complete, but my health had begun a rapid decline.

I remember the days of raising three young children and my husband arriving home to find me in tears because I didn't think I could adequately take care of them. As the kids grew and were off to school, I remember setting my alarm clock to make sure I would get out of bed and not forget to pick them up. I remember the days my husband would come home and have to cook, clean, and help with the laundry. I remember friends calling and wanting to do things. I would turn them down time and time again until I had pushed everyone that ever meant anything to me out of my life. I remember not being able to plan trips because, inevitably, I would end up sick or with a migraine. I remember not being able to schedule having anyone over for dinner because I didn't know from one minute to the next how I would be feeling. I remember struggling through the holidays, trying to make them special for the children, but secretly dying through the pain. I remember asking God to take me home and to spare my family from further burden.

The feelings were deep and very real.

The feelings were deep and very real. I was in pain. I was a mess. I was failing as a wife and as a mom. It was all I could do to get out of bed in the morning. I was blessed with an amazing, supportive husband and three strong children; however, I knew in my heart I was falling short of my responsibilities in every way. I could barely show my love to my family as I hated myself and was falling deeper into depression.

I remember my oldest child—my beautiful, brilliant firstborn, Ariana—coming into my room each morning. She would attempt to wake me up to drive she and her two younger siblings to school. She would gently shake me, and I would cry out like a toddler throwing a tantrum, burying my face in my pillow, "*Nooooo!* I don't want to get up!" I would eventually drag myself out of bed, often driving the kids to school in my pajamas, plagued with the guilt of embarrassing them when one of their friends would run up to our car to greet us.

I remember the days of pain when I could not even carry the groceries up the steps from the garage to the kitchen. I would literally drag myself with one small bag of groceries at a time, get to the top of the stairs, fall to my knees, and cry out to God. I would yell at the top of my lungs, "*I hate my life!*"

Some of you, reading these all-too-familiar words, know exactly where I am coming from. You are currently engaged in your own secret battle of survival, wondering when it will all end—wondering if the pain will ever stop or if it will take you out. Please know that God hears your cries. He sees your pain. He is catching your every tear in a bottle. He loves you and has plans for you. He has not turned His face from you nor has He forsaken you.

Today I look back and rejoice at how far God has brought me. To think that only a few short years ago, I was miserable, taking ten prescription medications, in daily pain, hated my life, and just wanted to die.

Today, my life is full, overflowing with joy and peace, and I could not be more fulfilled.

God transformed me when He took me from the pit of despair to being healed of chronic disease. To date I have been healed of Hashimoto's thyroiditis, Sjögren's syndrome, fibromyalgia, chronic fatigue syndrome, reflex sympathetic dystrophy, and migraine headaches. I am in awe of my God who loves me, and I write this testimony to give you hope and encouragement despite your pain. My God does not show favoritism (Acts 10:34), and He will do for you what He has done for me. Oh how He loves you! Cling to that promise of hope as God leads you through your own journey to freedom from chronic illness.

CHAPTER 4

Words of Life

One day when I was home alone, defeated and praying to God, I received the sweetest phone call from my son. Brennan was a twenty-year-old college student studying abroad in Puerto Rico for the semester. He called to tell me that God had spoken to him, telling him he needed to come home. Brennan did not know how bad my physical condition had become because I tried to protect him from the harsh reality when he was so far away. I argued with him that it was the middle of the semester, that he was having the adventure of a lifetime, and that he needed to stay. He told me he had already purchased his plane ticket home and had it all arranged to finish his classes online. Little did I know how much I would come to rely on my precious son in the months ahead.

He knew my needs before I did...

Brennan ended up driving me to doctor appointments, to the pharmacy for prescriptions, to physical therapy three times a week, and everywhere else that I needed to go. One day as we were in the car, he said, "Mom, what would you have done had I not come home?" I had no idea how to answer that question except to say that God knew my needs. He had prepared the way for my son to take care of me so my husband could continue working. I was beginning to understand how much God actually loved me. To think He had arranged all of this ahead of time! He knew my needs before I did, and His faithfulness was overwhelming. I found myself reflecting on Matthew 6:8 which says, "...your Father knows exactly what you need even before you ask Him!" (NLT).

While Brennan was home, he was asked to speak at the North County Healing Rooms in the city where we resided. Being the good mom that I always tried to be, I dragged myself out of bed to go hear him. I did not feel well and sat in back, hoping to not be noticed by anyone. I was in pain. I just wanted to listen to my son and then get out of there, back to the comfort and safety of my bed… which I had grown to love a little too much.

Brennan finished speaking, and there was a time of ministry where people were praying for one another. I remember being in a really bad place, hoping no one would talk to me. I had been prayed for so many times to no avail, and I just wanted to get home. I had to wait for Brennan, so I put my head down pretending to pray, attempting to be invisible. As my eyes were closed and my head bowed, I became aware that someone sat down in the chair next to me. I actually prayed that this person would leave me alone and just go away. Instead, she did the unspeakable! This quiet soul placed her hand on my shoulder and began interceding for me. I did not open my eyes and, to this day, I do not know who this person was. She went on to speak words to me that only God and I knew. I began to weep. I could not believe that the God of the universe had sent this faithful, obedient woman to speak life and love into my spirit, soul, and body.

Here is a portion of what she said. As you read it, imagine me decreeing it over you. This is a NOW word to build hope and faith in your spirit:

> You are stepping into a new season. The past is gone. The Lord has not forgotten you. He has caught every one of your tears in a bottle. He wants you to know He has taken your baggage. It is His, and it is gone. He has given you a brand-new set of luggage that is your future. It is bright and new, full of hope and promise. He has wonderful things planned for you that you only need to step into. Quit looking back. There is no regret, no shame, and no unforgiveness. He took all of that when He died on the cross. Your future is full of life, and peace, and hope. Take the new luggage He has lovingly packed for you, open it, and begin using it.

I was in awe that God had sent this perfect stranger to speak His heart into my life. For the first time in a long time, I felt the tangible love of God. I thought, *Maybe He hasn't forgotten me. Maybe He hasn't turned His face from me.* I went home and pondered all that had taken place. Another step of healing in my soul had begun.

I want to stop here to tell you that God hasn't forgotten you! He hasn't turned His face from you. Trust me, He is working all things out for your good and for His glory. You may not be able to see it yet, but hold on because His promises *will* come to pass in your life. One day very soon, you are going to be writing your own chapter in your own book about the faithfulness of God in your life.

> *God hasn't forgotten you!*

I did not return to the Healing Rooms until the next summer when my son came home from another semester of school on the East Coast. He was asked to speak again, so I went. Once more, a total stranger came up to me and gave me a word from the heart of God. I was intrigued and thought, *There is something special about this place. There is something special about these people.* I began attending meetings at the Healing Rooms on occasion. Every time I showed up, somebody would pray for me or speak a word of encouragement to me. God was pursuing me in such a personal, passionate way. He was using His children to breathe life back into my weary body.

I began to hunger to spend time with God as I had in my early years of being a Christian. I pored over my Bible. I prayed. I listened to worship music. I could not get enough. I began picking out Bible verses on healing, reading about my identity as a child of God, and speaking the Scriptures out loud over my life. Other people began speaking God's Word over my life too. I was literally being brought back to vibrancy by the written and spoken Word of God. My heavenly Father was reaching into the depths of my soul, and the wounds of my heart were being healed. The illnesses I had been diagnosed with began dropping off of my body one by one. But this was only the beginning.

Are you ready for your own new beginning? God has been pursuing you since the day you were born. He has the most amazing plan for your life. He has an adventure awaiting you like no other you have ever been on! God is gentle and patient. He is exceedingly kind and will work things out at a pace He knows you can handle. Sometimes the journey is slow, when deemed necessary, but He always responds with patience and love for you. He is full of mercy and grace. Hold on! Your day is coming.

CHAPTER 5

Bitterness, Anger, and Unforgiveness

As God began my healing process, He began working from the inside out. I grew up around much negativity. People around me were always speaking negative things. I was an extremely sensitive child, and now, as an adult, I was beginning to recognize the power those words had held over me my entire life. Those words defined who I had become. When I was a little girl and would voice a hurt, concern, or pain, I was often told by well-meaning adults around me, "Oh that's all in your head," "That's ridiculous," or "That's crazy." I began believing that I was crazy, that my feelings were not normal and had to be buried.

Most of the adults involved in my upbringing focused extensively on the outward appearance. You had to look good. You had to be thin. You had to have

BITTERNESS, ANGER AND UNFORGIVENESS

money. You had to be successful. That was all I knew to strive for and I never felt good enough. I quickly learned that I had to act out to get attention. I never felt accepted. I began begging for attention even if it was negative attention. After all, negative attention was better than no attention at all.

As an adult in my early fifties, and for the first time in my life, I was feeling the unconditional love of God being manifested through my new friends. These women at the Healing Rooms were becoming dear to my heart. They were accepting me with all of my flaws, illnesses, insecurities, and problems. I was a mess when I came to them, but they loved me anyway. They spoke nothing but the heart of God to my soul. It was refreshing and new, and it was birthing something tangible inside of me.

As my heart began the healing process, God began speaking to me about deep-rooted issues that I needed to let go of. He was bringing to light the negative thought patterns, the deep-rooted anger, and the unforgiveness I had been holding on to. I had always pictured myself as a forgiving person, but I soon realized that though I had been saying, "I forgive," I was not feeling it nor taking it to heart.

One day at the Healing Rooms, a sweet, elderly woman named Nellie, who was in her eighties and full of life, energy, and vitality, came up to me and asked if she could pray for me. As she prayed, she recited 2 Corinthians 10:4–5 over me:

> For the weapons of our warfare *are* not carnal but mighty in God for pulling down strongholds, casting down arguments and every high

thing that exalts itself against the knowledge of God, bringing every thought into captivity to the obedience of Christ. (NKJV)

I was beginning to understand the power that these saints of old carried as they memorized the Word of God, believed it, lived by it, spoke it, and used it to breathe life into others. They had a secret weapon, and they were using it to live a vibrant life of faith in a real God who still cares about His people.

As I began poring over these verses, I realized that my thoughts were extremely negative. If my husband was a few minutes late arriving home from work, my mind would imagine him dead on the side of the road. If the doctor told me my labs were a little elevated and I needed further testing, I would immediately assume I was dying of cancer. If someone spoke a critical word to me, my thoughts rapidly went to, *She hates me.* I reached the point of trusting no one and nothing.

As I began meditating on the Word of God, it began taking root. It began transforming me. The Bible teaches in Hebrews 4:12 that:

> ...the Word of God is alive and active. Sharper than any double-edged sword, it penetrates even to dividing soul and spirit, joints and marrow; it judges the thoughts and attitudes of the heart.

The Word literally began judging the thoughts and attitudes of my heart. My thoughts were not good. They were partnering with the devil, and I needed some real transformation. I began to take every negative thought captive and give it to God. At first, it seemed I had to do it every five seconds. Within a month, I was becoming a new creation. My heart was being filled with joy and peace.

Whenever a person offended me, I immediately and verbally began giving my hurts and thoughts to God and actively forgiving the offense. I began to understand that when a person spoke something negative to me or offended me in some way, it usually wasn't about me at all. Often people react or say things in the heat of the moment because of how they are feeling about themselves at the time. Sometimes they react inappropriately due to how their day is going. You have probably heard the saying, "Hurting people hurt people." When somebody lashes out at you or responds to you in a manner that wells up any form of negativity, offense, fear, or hurt, it is often because they themselves are having a bad day. You may never really know what is going on behind the scenes.

Within a month, I was becoming a new creation.

A person may be grieving the loss of a relationship. They may be experiencing financial difficulties or problems at work. They may be struggling with their spouse or one of their children. They may be suffering from pain or illness. As I began to understand this concept, I began responding instead of reacting. I was able to reply in kindness and love rather than getting angry and snapping back.

I also stopped listening to the news. I was tired of hearing the gloom and doom that reporters were giving. I began listening to God and hearing what He was saying about the state of the world. I even stopped reading the posts of people who were posting negative things on social media. If I read something and it made negativity well up within me, I got rid of it. As I began cleansing my mind, I found myself trusting again, loving again, and living again. The bitterness and anger from my past were beginning to melt away. My heart wounds were being healed.

What are some tangible changes you can begin making today? Ask the Lord to reveal the things He would like to bring to the surface in your own life so He can begin the cleansing and purifying process. It may be painful at first, but the end results will definitely be worth it. There is no better time to begin than today!

CHAPTER 6

The Change

The Lord was doing a multifaceted work in me. I was beginning to understand that we are complex beings. We live *in* a body, we *have* a soul (made up of our mind, will, and emotions), yet we live *as* a spirit. A miracle was occurring in my body as my soul wounds were being addressed. The Lord was speaking to my heart and restoring my identity in Him. I had strayed way off course through the years of pain and suffering. I had bought into the lie that was an all-out assault to get me derailed from the plans God had for me.

Each of us is born with a call on our lives, a purpose, and a destiny to fulfill.

Each of us is born with a call on our lives, a purpose, and a destiny to fulfill. As the beautiful men and women of God at the North County Healing Rooms began speaking the Scriptures over my life, my true identity as a child of the Living God was being restored.

I was beginning to remember who I was and that God had plans for me. I was not just dropped here on this earth to suffer and endure a cruel existence. There was much more ordained for my life and I was determined to step into it. The Lord highlighted another verse for me from Jeremiah 29:11, "'For I know the plans I have for you,' declares the LORD, 'plans to prosper you and not to harm you, plans to give you hope and a future.'" I was actually becoming excited about my future for the first time in decades.

Simultaneously, God led me to a new chiropractor, Dr. Ryan McGaughey, who shared a practice with his wife, Dr. Carolyn, a naturopathic doctor. As he taught me about nutrition and about the thyroid function, I made changes to my diet and began taking supplements to support my body's natural defense mechanism. I had tried this before, but somehow this time it was different. I began learning about God's timing. When He wants us to make a change, He orchestrates things in numerous areas of our lives at the same time. He also gives a divine grace to accomplish what He is calling us to. At times, God requires things of us that are character building or just plain good for our body, soul, and spirit. I was convicted that the world as a whole was entering into an amazing new season in which we each needed to be strong, spiritually and physically.

Within three weeks of making both physical and spiritual changes, all of my fibromyalgia symptoms disappeared. I was no longer experiencing daily pain and had more energy than I had felt in years. I went from needing ten to twelve hours of sleep at night, plus a nap, to sleeping only seven to eight hours a night and never needing a nap. It was miraculous! I began praising God that He had healed me so dramatically of fibromyalgia and chronic fatigue syndrome. I was able to begin exercising regularly, which I had not been able to do in years. My doctor was amazed.

I began testifying of my healing to everyone I met. I was in awe of a God who loved me and had never turned His face from me, though He had felt distant and uncaring for many years. He continued to speak words of life to me through His written Word and through others who would speak Scripture and prophetic words over me. I was being told things such as, "God is going to give you back all the years the locusts have eaten" from Joel 2:25, and "God is going to restore everything the enemy has taken from you. Everything is going to be accelerated for you." As I took each word to heart, meditated on the Scriptures spoken over me, and prayed, God began aligning my heart with His. I was coming to know God as my Father for the very first time. I had a shaky relationship with my earthly father, who passed away many years ago, and I was beginning to understand that often our relationship with our earthly father is how we view our heavenly Father. For the first time in my life I was experiencing perfect love from my Father God as I had never known or felt it before.

Several months later, I found myself having fewer migraine headaches. When they did come, they were less severe and much farther apart. After twenty-plus years of migraines, this was miraculous in itself. I began praising God for each new victory. My vitality was returning, and I was feeling younger and more energized with each new day. I was no longer taking pain medication and began reducing all of my other daily medications. I continued testifying of His goodness. I was overcoming more and more of the devil's attack on my life as I surrendered and shared with others the goodness and faithfulness of the Lord. The verse "They triumphed over him [the enemy] by the blood of the Lamb and by the word of their testimony" (Revelation 12:11) became strength to my soul.

I remember the day I returned to the doctor who was managing my hypothyroid disease. It was time for my regular blood tests that I was required to repeat every six months. Each time my blood was checked, my numbers had gone up, resulting in a higher dose of thyroid medication year after year. For ten years my numbers had steadily climbed. This time however, the results came back clear, showing that I did not have Hashimoto's thyroiditis at all!

I began praising God for each new victory.

My doctor presumed there had been a mistake in the testing because, in his words, "You don't get better from Hashimoto's. There is no cure." He immediately provided me with a new lab order to have my blood re-tested. I willingly obliged. When the second test came back showing no signs of Hashimoto's, he was baffled but asked if we could test one more time. I agreed. When the third test results came back clear, there was nothing to say except that a miracle had taken place in my body! I asked permission to discontinue my thyroid medication, but he was hesitant and told me that I needed to wean off of it. We decided to reduce my dose each month until I was completely off of the medication. In six short months, I was entirely weaned and that was the last of my prescription medications.

It was strange to not be making weekly trips to the pharmacy, where they knew me on a first name basis.

I want to pause here and add that there is nothing you can do to earn your healing or your deliverance. It is only by the grace of God that we receive anything. There are no secrets, no magic formulas, and no step-by-step guides to follow. It was my time, and the Word of God was becoming life to my soul. It was a gift to receive, and I began to believe what the Word of God said about me. I began to make changes in my thought patterns and physical life. I needed healing for not only my body, but for my mind, will, and emotions as well, and it was coming. My healing was multi-faceted as I realized how much my poor physical health had been tied to my emotional health—holding onto unforgiveness, bitterness, and resentment, and entertaining negativity. I was learning that as I partnered with God and listened to His still, small voice, He was guiding my path to wholeness. He was restoring me to His perfect will.

James 1:2–4 says:

> Consider it pure joy, my brothers and sisters, whenever you face trials of many kinds, because you know that the testing of your faith produces perseverance. Let perseverance finish its work so that you may be mature and complete, not lacking anything.

Wow! I had never rejoiced in my trials and suffering, but I do now! I realize without a doubt that it was all a part of my maturing, becoming complete, lacking nothing. I praise God for all that I endured.

I would not be the person I am today without having gone through the valley of the shadow of death.

You, dear reader, are becoming a new person just by reading this book! You are on your own journey of healing. It is not an accident that you picked up this book at this moment in your life. God is orchestrating your steps and ushering in your healing. I encourage you to sit in the presence of God. Ask Him your questions. He will answer you in the most profound ways: through other people, through His Word as you pick up the Bible and read, through nature, and through hearing His still small voice. Jeremiah 33:3 says, "Call to me and I will answer you and tell you great and unsearchable things you do not know." The heart of the Father is to have a personal relationship with you, His precious child. "Come near to God and He will come near to you" (James 4:8).

CHAPTER 7

From Chronic Pain to Chronic Praise

Over a twelve-month period, I went from being on ten prescription medications down to zero. Every time I went back to the doctor, I received a new report. My doctors were baffled. They had not seen people cured of the things I was being healed of, yet the blood tests, symptoms, and results all pointed to the same prognosis. I was being healed! In Proverbs 18:21 it is written, "The tongue has the power of life and death." I had read this verse numerous times over the years, but this time God gave me a new revelation. For years, I had partnered with how I was feeling, with my symptoms, and with words well-meaning professionals were speaking over my life. I would state the obvious, "I am in pain. I am miserable. I have this or that disease." As the Lord gave me new insight into the power that my words held, I began speaking life over my body, spirit, and soul. As words of life were being spoken, I was being healed from the inside out, right before everyone's eyes, beginning with my soul wounds and wounds of the heart.

During this same period of time, I had been visiting a dear friend named Alma who resided in a nursing home. She was 104 years old and took no medication. It was unheard of for a woman this age to not be taking a single prescription. One day I asked her the secret to her health. I'll never forget the words she shared with me that day. "God spoke the world into being, and it was so. I speak the Word of God over my life each day, and it comes to pass." Then she began to recite from memory Psalm 103:1–5:

> Praise the LORD, my soul;
> all my inmost being, praise His holy name.
> Praise the LORD, my soul,
> and forget not all His benefits—
> who forgives all your sins
> and heals all your diseases,
> who redeems your life from the pit
> and crowns you with love and compassion,
> who satisfies your desires with good things
> so that your youth is renewed like the eagle's.

I went home that day and began memorizing those words of life.

I'll never forget the day I walked into my house carrying three bags of groceries up the staircase from the garage to the kitchen with ease. I flung open the door, dropped to my knees, and began to cry. But this time they were tears of joy! I had just proclaimed at the top of my lungs, "*I love my life!*" I instantly remembered the many trips up those very steps, dragging myself into the house, dropping to the floor, and crying out, "*I hate my life!*" I had come full circle.

My heart was becoming full of joy and peace. Nothing could shake me. Even when I received bad news, nothing seemed to rattle me. My emotions and thought patterns had become stable. Any time a negative thought or an old behavior tried to rear its ugly head, I threw Scripture at it. Isaiah 55:11 states, "So is My Word that goes out from My mouth: It will not return to Me empty, but will accomplish what I desire and achieve the purpose for which I sent it." Did you hear that? God's Word does not return void. It goes out and does what God purposes it to do. It has life-changing, transformational power!

Nothing could shake me.

I am in awe of how God reached out of heaven and touched me! He is a personal God. He does not love me more than you. What He has done for me, He will do for you! Believe! I know your faith is rising as you read these words. Let it rise up in your spirit! Let the life-changing Word of God bring health to your body! I have truly gone from chronic pain to chronic praise. I believe He will bring you to this place too. This is your day! This is your finest hour! God has a call on your life and a destiny for you to fulfill! He knew you in your mother's womb (Jeremiah 1:5). He knows the exact number of hairs on your head (Matthew 10:30, Luke 12:7). He has caught every one of your tears in a bottle (Psalm 56:8). This is how personal our God is. He desires an intimate relationship with you. He is a good and loving Father.

I want to stop and give praise and glory to God for the trials and tribulations He has so faithfully brought me through. Each of you has your own story. Some of these trials may resonate with you, and others may not. It is important to praise Him for every little victory along the way. Each time you have a breakthrough, stop and give Him honor and praise. He loves a heart of gratitude.

On a crisp November day a few years ago, I wrote in my journal:

- I used to need ten to twelve hours of sleep at night and still need a nap to make it through the day. Now I sleep just eight hours a night and wake up raring to go, full of energy, and super excited for all that God has for me each day!

- I used to not be able to go grocery shopping. I would cry out to God to help me carry the bags up the steps from my garage to my kitchen. I now race up the stairs with ease!

- I used to pray for a spot close to the store because I had no strength to walk. Now I walk with ease and even exercise vigorously at least five days a week!

- I used to have daily chronic fatigue and pain. Now I rarely have pain and am no longer fatigued. I feel younger than I have in twenty-five years! My youth is being renewed like the eagle's (Psalm 103:5).

- I used to hate getting up in the morning and arose with dread in my spirit. Now I wake up refreshed and with a song in my heart! I actually wake up singing!

- My husband used to have to carry the laundry up and down the stairs for me. I now carry the full baskets with ease!

- I used to suffer from ten to twelve migraines per month. Today I am free from migraine headaches!

- I used to crave sugar. Now I rarely crave sugar.

- My face was blotchy and full of acne. My face has improved tremendously!

- I used to not be able to memorize Scripture or anything else. My mind was forgetful. I now memorize Scripture regularly! I have a sound mind (2 Timothy 1:7).

- I used to not be able to pray out loud. I now pray boldly and with confidence!

- I used to have a competitive nature to a fault. The Lord has taught me what humility is and what it means to be last. I am content in my identity in Him and no longer have to strive to be the best at everything or try to be someone I am not. I *love* who I am in Him.

- I used to be jealous of everyone and everything. Now I am genuinely happy for others' successes, and I find joy in helping others become all that they were created to be!

- I never felt good enough or loved. I now know and feel deeply loved by my Father God.
- I used to get angry and often lost control of my tongue. I now exercise self-control, which is a fruit of the Spirit.
- I never used to take responsibility for my shortcomings. It was difficult to ask forgiveness of people. I was arrogant and full of pride. I was always on the defense. I now practice humility and am quick to ask forgiveness when I wrong others.
- I used to not be able to lift my left arm. I was in terrible pain and losing the use of the arm due to reflex sympathetic dystrophy. I now raise my arm in praise and worship daily!
- I used to love my bed. Now I love my life!
- I used to want to die. Now I am enjoying life to the fullest!

Wow! When I look back at how far God has brought me, I am in awe of His grace and mercy. He extends that same grace and mercy to you today. He loves you. You are beautiful in His sight. Begin to praise Him today. There is something you are grateful for. Even when everything is crumbling apart around you, you can find something to praise Him about. It may be a faithful loved one standing by your side. It may be that you have a warm bed to curl up in. It may be a roof over your head and food on your table. Begin to thank Him for *every* little thing. Soon you will be thanking Him for the **BIG** things!

> Do not be anxious about anything, but in every situation, by prayer and petition, with thanksgiving, present your requests to God. And the peace of God, which transcends all understanding, will guard your hearts and your minds in Christ Jesus. (Philippians 4:6–7)

Begin moving today
from chronic pain to chronic praise!

CHAPTER 8

Living Out the Call and Destiny

Today I am living the dream! I am living out the call and the destiny that God had for me from the beginning of time. I love my life, and I love who God made me to be. A few years before the writing of the first edition of this book, I could not say those words. I hated my life and wanted to die. I was jealous of everyone else's lives. The grass always looked greener in someone else's pasture. God brought amazing friends into my life who recognized my giftings and began celebrating my identity in Christ. They reminded me weekly of who God made me to be.

God began to show me that He made me to be *me*, not to be my friend who could sing the most melodic harmonies or my other friend who was the life of the party and lit up the room wherever she went.

I did not have to be another one of my friends who could pray the most powerful prayers I had ever heard. I finally understood that God made me to be me and nobody else. I am a unique creation to be celebrated as an individual child of God.

I know I still have a long way to go, but I rejoice in the plans God has for me. God is using me to restore hope to those who have no hope, to restore joy to those who have no joy, and to speak life to weary souls. God is using *me*! I never dreamed that I would be of use to God in my miserable, sickly state. Looking back, He always had a call on my life, as He does on yours! He was walking right beside me through the dark valley. He always intended to bring me back onto the mountaintop once again.

> *God made me to be me*

Even in my weakness, the testimonies began to emerge. One evening as my neighbors began fighting, I got a true taste as to how much the Lord was changing me. We happen to live near a family who has numerous problems. We often hear screaming and fighting coming from the home and yard. We know there are drugs, alcohol, and domestic violence involved. We have had to call the police on more than a few occasions. The "old" me used to lock the doors and windows and hide out in fear when I heard the fighting. The "new" me responded in confidence and love.

As the all too familiar shouting began, and foul language arose from the yard, I went outside and, from a distance, saw the neighbor man yelling and a woman crying. The mercy of God rose up within me and I got in my car and drove around to the front of their house. As I drove onto the driveway, I saw a young woman crouched in fear on the ground near a vehicle. She was sobbing. My neighbor, her boyfriend, was slamming a brick on the hood of her car over and over again, causing tremendous damage. I asked the Lord for wisdom and strength, then bravely stepped out of my car and walked up to the young man whom I had known since he was a little boy. He used to play with my son and was a sweet-natured child. I said, "Hey! Stop that! This is not who you are! You are a good man! You are kind! God did not make you to act this way! STOP!!!"

To be honest, I was terrified, thinking he might turn his anger on me and throw the brick my way. To my surprise, he stopped in his tracks and broke down crying. As I approached him, I placed my hand on his shoulder, and began praying for him out loud. I then explained that I was going to take his girlfriend, get in my car, and drive away with her. I told him he needed to cool down and talk to God about what he was feeling. I slowly backed away, helped the young woman up off of the ground, got her into my car, and drove her back to my house.

Inside the safety of my home, she poured out her story of loving my neighbor but feeling trapped in this abusive relationship. I shared the love of God with her and told her that He was the only one who was big enough to fix this mess. I led her in prayer to accept Jesus into her life and to ask for His help. She felt such peace after praying. We kept in close contact over the next several months. She was able to break off the relationship without any negative repercussions. Only God could have orchestrated that!

Living Out the Call and Destiny

The following week my husband and I made dinner and took it over to our neighbor and his father, who had recently been diagnosed with cancer. I was nervous, but knew God was in this. We knocked on the door and the neighbor answered. He was kind and pleasant and invited us in. We told him we had brought dinner and asked if we could pray for his father. His father looked weak and frail. They allowed us to pray for him. We could tell they were grateful. We know God allowed something to shift in their lives as we partnered with Him to bring His hope and love.

The Bible says in Philippians 4:13, "I can do all things through Him who gives me strength." God strengthens us to accomplish things that are out of our comfort zone and are not part of our normal personality. He is bigger than any crisis or illness we are facing. He had not only healed me, but He gave me purpose and a new outlook. He allowed me to be part of a story that had the potential to have a very negative ending. Instead, God filled me with boldness and used me to turn things around.

It was amazing to me that God didn't wait until I was totally healed and well to begin using me. As I began responding to the still small voice of the Father and heeding to His gentle promptings, He began to use me amidst all of my problems and weaknesses. God doesn't wait until we

> *"I can do all things through Him who gives me strength."*

are completely whole and well to use us. He will use you right where you are at if you surrender and say "Yes." 2 Corinthians 12:9-11 says:

"My grace is sufficient for you, for My power is made perfect in weakness." Therefore, I will boast all the more gladly about my weaknesses, so that Christ's power may rest on me. That is why, for Christ's sake, I delight in weaknesses, in insults, in hardships, in persecutions, in difficulties. For when I am weak, then I am strong.

If you are currently in the middle of your own crisis, don't despair and don't lose hope. God is with you. He sees your every tear. He will take your situation and turn it around for His glory if you allow Him to. Keep the faith. "Hope deferred makes the heart sick, but a desire fulfilled is a tree of life" (Proverbs 13:12). God wants you! God loves you! God wants to heal you. He is a good Father, and He is with you. Talk to Him about it. Surrender your life to the King of kings and the Lord of lords, Jesus Christ. Allow Him to begin using you even in your weakness. You have a call on your life. God has an incredible destiny for you. He has never given up on you. He has never turned His face from you. He has not forsaken you.

Father, I ask that You speak to the person reading this book right now. I ask that he hears Your voice clearly. I pray that You open her eyes to see and her ears to hear the plans You have for her. May he taste of Your kindness. May she walk in Your light. May You lift his burdens. May she experience who You really want to be for her. May he feel the tangible presence of a living God who loves him with a perfect, eternal love. May she smell Your sweet fragrance as she basks in Your presence. Illuminate all five senses and breathe

Your sons and daughters to life so that they may know of Your goodness and become Your hands and feet, bringing hope to this lost and hopeless world.

CHAPTER 9

He Hears the Cries of Your Heart

Does worry or stress plague you? Do anger and bitterness get the best of you? Do shame and guilt consume you? You are not alone. Most of the world deals with negative emotions on a daily basis. The difference is what you choose to do with them. You must stop entertaining the negative! If your upbringing had you around constant negativity, you will most likely operate with a negative mind-set as I did for most of my life.

I must confess that I have been a Christian for more than thirty years, and it has only been in the past five years that I have come to experience the peace and joy of God in all of my circumstances. I love to meditate on this Scripture from Philippians 4:8–9:

> Finally, brothers and sisters, whatever is true, whatever is noble, whatever is right, whatever is pure, whatever is lovely, whatever is admirable—if anything is excellent or praiseworthy—think about such things. Whatever you have learned or received or heard from me, or seen in me—put it into practice. And the God of peace will be with you.

This peace only comes from knowing Jesus. Some of you reading this book do not *know* Jesus. You may have grown up in church but never truly met Jesus. You may have never stepped foot inside of a church in your life, yet you know instinctively that there is more to this life. That is because you were created to have a personal relationship with a loving Savior. You were born with a call on your life. You were born to live out an extraordinary destiny that only *you* can fulfill.

I knew from the time I was a little girl that I was unique and made for something special, yet I did not personally meet the God of the universe until I was eighteen years old and living in a college dorm room three hours from my hometown. I had attended church my whole life, but I did not understand that there was a loving Father out there who sent His only Son to die on a cross to redeem me and to pay the price for my sins. I had read the Scripture from John 3:16 numerous times:

> **For God so loved the world that He gave His one and only Son, that whoever believes in Him shall not perish but have eternal life.**

I had even memorized it, but it meant nothing to me. It was not personal.

One cold winter evening, I entered my college dorm lobby after returning from a jog with a friend. There was an evangelist preaching about a living God who wanted a personal relationship with me. I stopped and listened, and for the first time in eighteen years, the Word of God became alive for me. My life was changed forever. I accepted Jesus into my heart and nothing was ever the same again. I stepped into eternal life with a loving Savior and a new best friend.

For the next three decades, the enemy of my soul, Satan, did everything he could to rob me of my destiny—of my purpose for being alive. Each year I walked further and further into sickness, weakness, disease, and the lies of the devil. He was stealing my identity right out from under me. It wasn't until I was at my lowest moment—the point of taking my own life—that God, in His infinite grace, stepped out of heaven and reached into my heart through people who loved Him. I heard His voice and acted in obedience so that my healing could begin. I was truly walking through the valley of the shadow of death that the famous Psalm 23 talks about. Yet my gracious, loving heavenly Father did not leave me there. He carried me through and brought me to the mountaintop again.

If you are still walking through your own dark valley, I want to pray for you now. My God is a loving Father who wants to breathe hope and new life into your weary, worn-out body. He wants to revive your soul and fill your spirit up to overflowing so that you are not just surviving but thriving.

He Hears the Cries of Your Heart

God, I ask You to do what You did for me for the person reading these words. You are no respecter of persons, and You love those who seek You with all their heart.

Open your heart today and say these words aloud:

Father God, I need You. I am at the end of my rope and can no longer hold on. Today I make a choice. I let go of the rope and surrender all to You. (Raise both hands up to Him in an act of surrender.) I surrender my hopes, my dreams, my fears, my pain, my sickness, and my life. I give it all to You. Change me. Make me new. Mold me and shape me into the person You planned for me to be from the time I was formed in my mother's womb. I don't want to walk this road alone any longer. Only You can meet my deepest needs, not another person, not fame, nor fortune, only an encounter with You, the Living God. Please forgive me for trying to do it on my own. Please forgive me for my sins. I accept Your son, Jesus, into my heart, whom You sent to die on a cross for my sins. Today is the beginning of the rest of my life. I am Yours. Use me for Your glory. In Jesus' name I pray. Amen.

If you sincerely prayed that prayer, rest assured that the God of the universe heard your words and saw your heart. You have been saved. You are God's child. You are now part of a family. The Word of God says, "If you declare with your mouth, 'Jesus is Lord,' and believe in your heart that God raised Him from the dead, you will be saved" (Romans 10:9).

I must pause here to impress upon your spirit that you are not only saved, but you are desperately needed. There are people out there in the world that are waiting to hear *your* unique story. They need what only *you* bring to the table. You may be thinking that you have nothing to offer or that you have messed up one too many times. I am here to tell you that is a lie!

The Bible says that God's mercies are new every morning (Lamentations 3:22–23, ESV). He does not want you looking back unless it is to forgive someone or to ask forgiveness. He wants you only looking forward into the plans and destiny that He has for you. Make this verse your own, "'For I know the plans I have for you,' declares the LORD, 'plans to prosper you and not to harm you, plans to give you hope and a future'" (Jeremiah 29:11). He does not promise that there won't be heartache or suffering, but He does promise to use it all for His glory in and through you. "For it is God who works in you to will and to act in order to fulfill His good purpose" (Philippians 2:13).

Today is the day of your new beginning. Your healing begins now. Deliverance is at hand. Today is the day of restoration and the beginning of the fulfillment of all of His promises in your life. No more will you smile on the outside yet feel as if you are dying on the inside. Joy and peace are yours. They are a gift from your heavenly Father who loves you so. Step into it, my friend, and don't look back! Today is the first day of the rest of your life. Today is the day of your destiny!

> *Today is the day of your new beginning.*

In the name and power of Jesus Christ, I break off of your life every yoke of fear, pain, anxiety, depression, illness, and despair. I speak to your body and command it to arise in hope, peace, and joy. May you experience the fullness of God as He rises up inside of you at this very moment. Holy Spirit, I ask You to fill Your precious sons and daughters to overflowing right now. Make them vessels of grace and mercy. Heal them and make them whole for the glory of God to be revealed in and through each one.

From this day forward, nothing but the blood of Jesus flows through your veins. His very DNA floods your body renewing and restoring EVERYTHING the enemy came in and stole from you. Today the reset button has been pressed and you are being *re-set* to the original factory settings that you were created for. Today begins the most amazing adventure of your lifetime. Today is the day of your salvation! Today is the day you become new and walk into your true destiny. Today you become everything the Word of God says about you. Today faith arises in your spirit and aligns with what the Holy Spirit wants to do in and through you.

> Brothers and sisters, I do not consider myself yet to have taken hold of it. But one thing I do: Forgetting what is behind and straining toward what is ahead, I press on toward the goal to win the prize for which God has called me heavenward in Christ Jesus. (Philippians 3:13-14)

Forget what lies behind! Press forward to the high calling of the Creator of the universe! Today the shift happens and you begin to walk into total transformation from the inside out.

CHAPTER 10

Total Transformation

Is total transformation possible? Only in Christ Jesus and the finished work of the cross. Once you have surrendered your life to Him, asked forgiveness for your sins, and accepted Him as your Lord and Savior, new life begins. The perfect blood of Jesus covers all of your sins and shortcomings, but it doesn't stop there. Read this incredible promise from Jesus found in John 14:12-17:

> I assure you: The one who believes in Me will also do the works that I do. And he will do even greater works than these, because I am going to the Father. Whatever you ask in My name, I will do it so that the Father may be glorified in the Son. If you ask Me anything in My name, I will do it. If you love Me, you will keep My commands. And I will ask the Father, and He will give you another Counselor to be with you

forever. He is the Spirit of truth. The world is unable to receive Him because it doesn't see Him or know Him. But you do know Him, because He remains with you and will be in you. (HCSB)

Jesus continues in verse 26 by stating:

But the Counselor, the Holy Spirit—the Father will send Him in My name—will teach you all things and remind you of everything I have told you. (HCSB)

Apart from Jesus, we can do nothing. With Him, we can do *all* things. If you want to walk in total transformation, it is important to receive the baptism of the Holy Spirit after giving your life to Jesus. I accepted Jesus into my heart when I was eighteen years old, but I struggled with old patterns and mindsets for the next thirty years. It seemed that just when I would make progress, I would have a setback and have to start over. This was a frustrating cycle. It wasn't until I acknowledged and received the gift of the Holy Spirit—whom Jesus sent to us when He returned to the Father—that I began to overcome the old behaviors that held me captive and kept setting me back year after year.

Receiving the baptism of the Holy Spirit is the key to living a fulfilling and adventurous life as a believer and follower of Jesus. In Acts 1:4–5, Jesus tells His disciples:

"…Wait for the gift my Father promised, which you have heard Me speak about. For John baptized with water, but in a few days you will be baptized with the Holy Spirit."

After they were baptized in the Holy Spirit, everything changed! Jesus indicated in Acts 1:8, "But you will receive power when the Holy Spirit comes on you; and you will be My witnesses in Jerusalem, and in all Judea and Samaria, and to the ends of the earth." All of a sudden, things shifted!

After receiving the Holy Spirit, weak, cowardly Peter, who had denied the Lord three times due to fear, was transformed into a strong, *bold* preacher of the Gospel. The people who heard Peter speak were astonished at his boldness. How could Peter, an uneducated fisherman, speak with such power and authority? He was no longer afraid of persecution! People saw the transformation in him. This ordinary disciple became an extraordinary man of God:

> When they saw the courage of Peter and John and realized that they were unschooled, ordinary men, they were astonished and they took note that these men had been with Jesus. (Acts 4:13)

That is the power of the baptism of the Holy Spirit! When we are filled with the Holy Spirit, we die to ourselves with all of our flaws and insecurities and become alive in God. It doesn't mean we suddenly all pack up and go off to seminary to become pastors, but rather, we become filled with courage and boldness outside of our normal personality to accomplish that which we were created to do.

Darkness and light cannot co-exist. Satan is dark and causes sin. God is light and pushes out the darkness. God and Satan cannot dwell in the same place. When you accept Jesus as your personal Lord and Savior and receive the infilling of the Holy Spirit, you will be changed forever. You will no longer desire the dark things of the world.

> Those who live according to the flesh have their minds set on what the flesh desires; but those who live in accordance with the Spirit have their minds set on what the Spirit desires. (Romans 8:5)

With the Holy Spirit living in you, you will no longer desire harmful, destructive behaviors. Your spirit will crave the things of God. You will genuinely desire to make a difference in the world and begin to go after the heart of the Father. Your life will be completely transformed as you enter the adventure of a lifetime serving the King of kings and bringing glory to His name.

With the Holy Spirit living in you, you will no longer desire harmful, destructive behaviors.

If you have not yet been baptized in the Holy Spirit, I would like to pray for you now. This is an opportunity to receive the power and boldness that came to the apostles in the upper room. This will change your life. No longer will you strive in the flesh to get it right. God will begin to work in and through you with the anointing He will impart from heaven. It will become second nature to live a supernatural life of righteousness, peace, and joy.

Please hold your hands out in a posture to receive:

Lord God, I pray for the ones reading these words right now to receive Your gift of the baptism of the Holy Spirit. As You did for me, please do for them to an even greater degree of anointing. As they open their mouths right now, fill them with Your heavenly language and give them a personal encounter with the Living God. Thank You that You are Lord. Thank You that You do not leave us alone to fend for ourselves when we know not how to pray. Thank You that You are God and we are not. We release all of our burdens to You, and we take Your yoke, for Your yoke is easy and Your burden is light (Matthew 11:30). Thank You that You are who You say You are, and that You do what You say You do. In Jesus' name we pray. Amen.

Don't wait another day!

- Begin the transformation from death to life…
- From sickness to health…
- From weakness to power in the Holy Spirit…
- From a life of chaos to a life of righteousness, peace, and joy…

This is what you were created for!
Don't wait another moment!
He is waiting for you.
Just say, "Yes Lord!!!"
Let the transformation begin!

To learn more about total transformation, read:

Strategies from Heaven, Contending for the Impossible

This book will provide you with hands-on strategies that you can immediately begin implementing to help you walk out the full call and destiny you were created for.

About the Author

Debbie Bilek is an author, coach, and motivational speaker. God has healed her of fibromyalgia, chronic fatigue syndrome, Hashimoto's thyroiditis, Sjögren's syndrome, migraine headaches, and reflex sympathetic dystrophy. Her passion is to see people healed, delivered, and restored to their true identity. She speaks the Word of God over lives with power and authority, imparting truth and transformation. She fuels others to live out their unique purpose and God-given destiny.

Debbie has been married for 32 years to her college sweetheart and the love of her life, Bill. Together they have three grown children who are destined to be world-changers.

To invite Debbie to share her testimony, speak, or minister at your event, you may contact her at:
info@StrategiesFromHeaven.com

For further resources visit:
StrategiesFromHeaven.com

www.ingramcontent.com/pod-product-compliance
Lightning Source LLC
LaVergne TN
LVHW021735060526
838200LV00052B/3294